The Missing Face

(new edition)

The Missing Face
(new edition)

Osonye Tess Onwueme

AFRICAN HERITAGE PRESS
NEW YORK • LAGOS • LONDON
2005

AFRICAN HERITAGE PRESS

NEW YORK   PO BOX 14452
PO BOX 1433   IKEJA
NEW ROCHELLE   LAGOS
NY 10802   NIGERIA

Library of Congress Control Number: 96-95387
Onwueme, Tess Osonye

[Selections: 2002]
The Missing Face/Tess Onwueme, new edition.
—Theatre and Drama, Literature, History, and Africana, Multicultural, Feminist and Gender Studies.

ISBN: 0-9628864-3-2

Dedicated

For the treasures of my life,

my children—

KENOLISA: Chukwu-Enwe-iwe-ka-madu, Uzodinma, Amaechi, Tokunbo, Chukwuma;

EBELE: Obi-Eluem-Ani, Ife-Chukwu-de, Uchenna, Elili-nma, Nwa-lokom-obi, Kika-Chukwu;

KUNUME: Uwa-ne-Kwu-nu-me, Kikiweji, Adanma, Enujeko, Naidene, Aka-onye-enyee, Chukwu-mon-nso;

BUNDO: Baabundo, Chukwu-eloke, Ose-emuchee, Emeka, Kikamme, Edidion, Ka-Chi-kwu;

MALIJE: Onye-Malije? Chiloe, Chim-Elozo-nam, Nwaka-ego, Ozili, Sisom-Awina, Nke-iru-ka, Eli-enye;

How can I tell you
That you are, each of you,
The very fountain of my life—
The meaning of all my struggles?

How can I tell you
That in you, I find the true meaning—
"Nne-Bu-Eze"...
Yes, **"Mother Is Gold"**!

But beneath it all,
"Nwa-Awodo"!

You, my children
Are my very life-essence—my life-support!

Can I thank you enough,
For unlocking the unwritten text
Of my Womanhood?

Other Creative Works By Osonye Tess Onwneme

Shakara: Dance-Hall Queen. San Francisco: African Heritage Press, 2000.
*Winner, the 2001 Association of Nigerian Authors (ANA) Drama Prize.

Why The Elephant Has No Butt. San Francisco: African Heritage Press, 2000.

Tell It To Women. Detroit: Wayne State University Press, 1997.
*Winner, the 1995 Association of Nigerian Authors (ANA) Drama Prize.

Riot In Heaven. San Francisco: African Heritage Press, 1997.

The Missing Face. San Francisco: African Heritage Press, 1996.

Three Plays. Detroit: Wayne State University Press, 1993.

Legacies. Ibadan: Heinemann Nigeria Ltd., 1989.

The Reign of Wazobia. Ibadan: Heinemann Nigeria Ltd., 1988.

Mirror for Campus. Ibadan: Heinemann Nigeria Ltd., 1987.

Ban Empty Barn & Other Plays. Ibadan: Heinemann Nigeria Ltd., 1986.

The Desert Encroaches. Ibadan: Heinemann Nigeria Ltd., 1995.
*Winner, the 1985 Association of Nigerian Authors (ANA) Drama Prize.

The Broken Calabash. Ibadan: Heinemann Nigeria Ltd., 1984.

A Hen Too Soon. Owerri: Heins Nigeria Publishers, 1983.

Recent Production History
of the Drama

Although other editions of this play have been staged in several (con)texts in Africa, and especially in Nigeria, the international premiere of this North American edition of *The Missing Face* was featured in a brilliantly memorable Off-Broadway performance, from April 27-May 28, 2001, at the Woodie King. Jr.'s NEW FEDERAL THEATRE, starring the following cast in order of appearance:

Stephanie Berry	Ida Bee
Angeline Butler	Nebe
William J. Marshall	Odozi
Kim Sullivan	Momah
Tobias Truvillion	Amaechi
David Wright	Afuzue/Griot

Directed by Pat White, the show featured the following technical crew:

Bukanla	Production Stage Manager
Antoinette Tynes	Lighting Designer
Anita D. Ellis	Costume Designer
David D. Wright	Sound Designer
Terry Chandler	Set Designer

Critical Acclaim for
Osonye Tess Onwueme

In all her work, Onwneme has shown daring in her exploration of ideas, even when they lead to subjects and themes which may seem taboo. She has a way of using images to express very crucial ideas. For example, in Legacies [or The Missing Face]—where Ikenga is split into two halves— she explores important pan-African themes and sums up the historical tragedy of the first major division of Africa into continental and diasporan entities. Wholeness will come when the two halves come together.
Ngugi wa Thiong'o, foreword to Onwueme's Tell It To Women.

'The Missing Face is Beholding'...In this meticulously paced play, Ida...a true optimist about love, family and her culture, takes a great leap in rearing her son, Amaechi...until she decides to leave the masculine formation of her young man-child to his father, who is domiciled in Africa...'The Missing Face' offers a rich illustration of music...ritual and tradition that is noble in looking back and seizing the moment.
Laura Andrews, Amsterdam News, New York.

For one month, the world famous Woodie King. Jr.'s NEW FEDERAL THEATRE...is presenting THE MISSING FACE, written by multi-award winning Nigerian writer, Tess Onwueme, presently the Distinguished Professor of Cultural Diversity & Professor of English at the University of Wisconsin, Eau Claire, Wisconsin. This exciting and challenging work demands two things from its audience: an ability to hear the fresh poetry of life, rolling in accents heightened by African dancing, chanting, and drumming, and an active imagination...This magnificent piece needs to be seen by audiences everywhere because the issues raised and answered are universal. They are issues affecting every human being today who is under siege by an inhumane, spiritless and materialistic society. And for all societies the answers will be the same: FIND your Missing Face.

Laurence Holder, Playwright/Professor at CUNY, New York City.

About the Author

Born in Nigeria, Osonye Tess Onwueme has established a significant reputation as the leading African female playwright, with international distinctions in Africa, North America, and Europe. After her BA and MA degrees from the University of Ife, Nigeria, she earned her Ph.D. in Literature from the University of Benin, Nigeria. In both the year, 2000 and 2001, she was awarded substantial grants for her creative writing and production by the Ford Foundation. From April 27-May 28, 2001, *The Missing Face* was featured in the highly acclaimed, Off-Broadway performance at the Woodie King Jr.'s New Federal Theatre in New York City. In addition, her scintillating drama, *Shakara: Dance-Hall Queen*, won the 2001 Association of Nigerian Authors (ANA) Drama Prize, which she had won with two earlier plays, *Tell it To Women* (1995), and *The Desert Encroaches* (1985).

Furthermore, she has won the following prestigious awards for her writing: the 1988 Distinguished Authors Award, the 1989/90 Martin Luther King, Jr./Caesar Chavez Distinguished Writers Award, the 1993 Nigerian Eagles Award, the 1994 Achievement Award in Literature, and the 1995 University of Wisconsin Award for Excellent Contributions by Women of Color to the University System.

In addition to her novel, *Why the Elephant Has No Butt* (2000), the writer also has these plays to her credit: *The Broken Calabash* (1984), *A Scent of Onions* (1986), *Ban Empty Barn and Other Plays* (1986), *Mirror for Campus* (1987), *Riot In Heaven* (1996), and *Then She Said It!* (2002). In 1994, she joined the University of Wisconsin, Eau Claire, Wisconsin as the first Distinguished Professor of Cultural Diversity, and Professor of English. Other international institutions she has taught include: Vassar College, Poughkeepsie, New York, Montclair State University, Montclair, New Jersey, Wayne State University, Detroit, Michigan, the University of Ife, Federal University of Technology, Owerri, and Imo State University, Nigeria.

About the Play

The Missing Face dramatizes the conflicts involved with personal and collective survival and renewal. Like the archetypal **Sankofa bird** (which must strain her neck to reach back and retrieve the egg left behind), IDA BEE, an African American woman, takes her teenage son, AMAECHI, on a very tedious journey, back to their ancestral roots in the African kingdom of Idu. Their primary quest is to find AMAECHI's father, MOMAH, who had abandoned them in Milwaukee after his studies in the USA to return to his African homeland. Having "lived from pay-check to pay-check", with the insecure, run-down inner city neighborhood, where the black men are increasingly being incarcerated in prisons that are often fed by crime, unemployment, racial, gender, and class crises, IDA BEE decides to find her son's father so that he, too, does not end up like other kids from the broken families in Milwaukee. Above all, she wants to provide a strong family base to secure her son's sense of manhood, identity and pride.

On this mythical journey, IDA BEE and AMAECHI carry with them the heavy burden of the split "Ikenga". The "Ikenga" signifies the Igbo ancestral symbol of manhood and personal achievement. This split "Ikenga" had been passed down from previous generations of her family in the diaspora, and her own father had given it to her on her twenty-first birthday, with the injunction that she must **"find the missing half of the face"**.

Although IDA BEE's journey to Idu with her son is remarkably heightened, lightened and sustained by music, dance, and the rich poetic lore of the black folk wisdom, their search weighs heavily on those who experience it with them. What will they discover as they enter into the throbbing heart of Africa? Will this search open up the old wounds of history to reveal the hidden faces and mysteries of the past that had long eluded and confounded them in the diaspora, with their estranged family in the African continent? And if the African Americans arrive in Idu, will their people recognize them? Will the African "drums" welcome them? What will the "drums" say to them? Will they find the other half of the "missing face" which has burdened the entire black race for centuries? And if they do, how will their finding awaken a new consciousness of selfhood and history within the peasants of Idu in the continent? These are some of the burning questions that inflame and invigorate the odyssey and mythological quest of these peoples of African descent. Here, the personal becomes the collective, and the mundane becomes the archetypal human struggle for recovery, renewal and rebirth in *The Missing Face*.

The Missing Face

CAST OF CHARACTERS

IDA BEE:
(36 years old): African American woman in her journey back to her ancestral roots in Africa.

AMAECHI:
(17 years old): IDA BEE's son. "AMAECHI" — "Who knows tomorrow?"

MOMAH:
(40 years old): IDA BEE's African husband. Later MOMAH and IDA BEE discover that they are brother and sister. "Momah" — "The Ancestors/Gods Know."

ODOZI:
(76 years old): MOMAH's uncle, a blacksmith, hunter and farmer. "Odozi" — "The One Who Mends."

NEBE:
(56 years old): Mother to MOMAH and wife to ODOZI. "Nebe" — "We Watch The World."

AFUZUE/GRIOT:
The Historian/Griot/ Story Teller. He plays the role of kinsman, drummer. towncrier, and the lead-chorus of Idu. "Afuzue" — "The Eye has Seen it All."

CHORUS OF IDU:
Men, Women and Children of Idu Kingdom.

1

Movement One

(Time present, midnight. Patches of dark clouds hanging as if suspended by the fingers of an emerging, crescent moon. Drums, throbbing in the heart of the land. A cast of round mud huts, crowned with conical thatch-roofs stand defiant, confronting the face of the modern mansions ahead of them, and outside the rustic ambiance of this present state. At the center of these huts the eye is struck by the regal eminence of one particular hut. This hut is beaded with cowrie-shells draped around it, its front door embroided with red eagle feathers. This is ODOZI's compound. ODOZI is the blacksmith, hunter and farmer. He is also MOMAH's uncle and the Diopka, elder or father of Idu kingdom. Prominent in this compound is the [1] "Ogwa," as the communal grotto/shrine with the double-faced ancestral mask, wearing extensive, long rafia "beards" from jaw to toe as its distinctive feature. Standing, resplendent in the lower right, and a little away from the grotto/shrine is a loom with colored threads and some designs in the making. On the lower left is the blacksmith's forge with tools and metals hanging above the bellows, and with scraps in the making on the other side. The heart of the land continues throbbing with the rhythm of drums. Soon, voices flow into the rhythms and amplify them until they stop suddenly as two other strange voices emerge and gain prominence among the rhythms in the grotto/shrine. It is IDA BEE and her teenage son, AMAECHI. They look burdened by the weight of their baggage. In spite of this sagging load which they try so much to adjust, they appear fascinated by the ritual power of this environment. AMAECHI is visibly weighed down by his own burden and soon loses interest. Tired, weary and frustrated, he throws his bag on the floor and slumps down.)

IDA BEE:
Uh, uh—Pick it up.

AMAECHI:
I'm tired Mama.

IDA BEE:
Tired? We just got started.

AMAECHI:
I'm tired and I don't want to go any further.

IDA BEE:
You want to stop now after coming this far?

AMAECHI:
Mama, I'm tired. I'm tired of the whole trip.

IDA BEE:
Pick up the bag Amaechi. We've got a lot of ground to cover before it gets dark.

AMAECHI:
We ain't got no business out here in the jungle mama, and you know it.

IDA BEE:
Amaechi, we've been through all this before.

AMAECHI:
I don't get it. What do you hope to find out here?

IDA BEE:
Our place in the world.

AMAECHI:
Our place is back in Milwaukee, not Africa.

IDA BEE:
How many times have I got to tell you that the homeland of black people is Africa, not Milwaukee?

AMAECHI:
Mama, I was born black in Milwaukee, not Africa. So don't confuse me.

IDA BEE:
Are you confused child?

AMAECHI:
(Irritably.) I'm tired. Tired of messin' around out here and gettin' no place.

IDA BEE:
(Exasperated.) What do you know about gettin' anyplace? I'm the one who works from paycheck to paycheck in an empty job goin' nowhere. Nike shoes and video games—bills piling up before I even

3

earn the money. Hate to see the mailman comin'. There's got to be more to life than payin' bills. That's why we must find our place in the world. A place where we can be whole ... a place that can fill the emptiness with kinship and the spirit of our ancestors.

AMAECHI:
What kind of kinship you talkin' about Mama?

IDA BEE:
Family.

AMAECHI:
Only family I know is in Milwaukee. We got Uncle Henry and Uncle Ron and Aunt Kathie and Aunt Gloria. They're my people. We know them. They know us. But nobody knows us here. We're strangers to them, and they're strangers to us. So, we don't belong here! Ma, let's go back to Milwaukee, where we belong ... where we know somebody.

IDA BEE:
All we got in Milwaukee is a bunch of fractured lives. Uncle Henry is an alcoholic. His wife and children livin' up in Kenosha with Uncle Ron, whose little Oshkosh job can hardly feed himself, let alone some extra mouths. And Uncle Charlie? Well, you know Uncle Charlie. So slick he can't keep himself out of jail. And Aunt Gloria is alone. She's got seven children and she's alone and don't even know it. Alone with no place in the world. And Uncle Mikey, the baby in the family, who carried so much promise for us, went off to college, got himself a big time corporate job and forgot all about us when he hit the Big Apple.

AMAECHI:
And that's why you wanted me to stay in school?

IDA BEE:
I was tryin' to keep your butt out of jail, boy.

AMAECHI:
I told you, Ma, the gun didn't belong to me.

IDA BEE:
It was in your possession.

AMAECHI:
I was holdin' it for Jay Jay, that's all. Wasn't gonna do nothin' with it.

IDA BEE:
Then why did you show it off in the school yard?

AMAECHI:
I told you. This girl wanted to see it. She didn't believe I had enough nerve to carry a gun.

IDA BEE:
And what did that prove?

AMAECHI:
I just wanted to show her I was a man.

IDA BEE:
A man? Is that all it takes to be a man? Showin' off your pistol?

AMAECHI:
You need a gun out there, Ma. Everybody got their own gun but me.

IDA BEE:
And what would you do with a gun?

AMAECHI:
I don't know.

IDA BEE:
Shoot somebody, that's what you would do.

AMAECHI:
If they mess with me, I'd have to.

IDA BEE:
And that's all it takes to be a man? Shoot somebody?

AMAECHI:
I wasn't gonna shoot nobody, mama. I swear, I was just holdin' the gun for Jay when Linda got all up in my face and said, "Aw, I don't believe you some kind of man that can hold a gun." I had to show her, Ma. That's all, just show her.

5

IDA BEE:
When we find your father, he's gonna teach you what a real man is all about.

AMAECHI:
I ain't got no father.

IDA BEE:
You do, too.

AMAECHI:
Ain't none of the kids on my street got a father.

IDA BEE:
Your father is here in Africa.

AMAECHI:
He sure ain't in Milwaukee, so I don't see what he can teach me.

IDA BEE:
He can teach you that an African man carries the power of the gun in his heart, then walks boldly through the forest of demons with a steady stride, his feet planted firmly on the ground like an elephant, trampling vipers and scorpions that threaten his progress toward the light of the sun.

AMAECHI:
I wouldn't know such a man if I saw him.

IDA BEE:
Such a man would know you, though.

AMAECHI:
Then how come he left us? It's been ten years since he laid eyes on us. We could pass each other in this night without ever knowing it.

IDA BEE:
Blood has a way of coming together like the tributaries of a river. You could never be a stranger to the man who named you, "Amaechi"— "who knows tomorrow?" *(She stops down to cajole him.)* Now, why don't you stop acting ugly and be beautiful for your Mama.

AMAECHI:

(Resisting.) Let's go home, Mama.

IDA BEE:

(Vexed.) Boy, pick up the bag.

AMAECHI:

It's heavy.

IDA BEE:

Of course it's heavy, that's why you're carrying it!

AMAECHI:

(Standing, lifting the bag and staggering.) Don't know why I've got to lug this thing around anyway.

IDA BEE:

Thing ... ? You call what you're carrying "a thing". Open up the bag. Go on, open it. Take out this "Thing" you call a "Thing".

(AMAECHI opens the bag and brings out an image which he looks at in disgust. IDA BEE snatches it from him.)

IDA BEE:

Now, look at it closely. How many times have I got to tell you that this object you call a "Thing" is your legacy? It's the split image of the [2]"Ikenga" of our people. It was passed down from my great-grandfather to my grandfather, onto my father who gave it to me on my 21st birthday. It was all that was left behind when Daddy lost his job, went out in search of work and never returned, leaving me and mother alone with memories. Daddy's last words were, "Hold on to this Ikenga. Some day, you will mend the splinted face of our people, and we'll be whole again." (She grows passionate and begins singing the blues while still trying to hold onto her son and to cajole him into joining her song. Slowly, but steadily, AMAECHI unwinds and joins her song which they sing together, and still holding onto each other until the end.) So now AMAECHI, the legacy is as much your burden as it is mine. Now pick it up and put it away. I hear voices ... (They break up and stay on the alert.)

7

Movement Two

(AMAECHI takes the mask from her and is about *to put it away when members of the community overwhelm the scene with their ritual dance, music and song. IDA BEE and AMAECHI retreat to the back of the grotto. They watch the ritual with keen interest and the lead dancer with great admiration as the community sings and chants. The song is *"Meme"—see the appendix. IDA BEE and AMAECHI come to a freeze beside the grotto, watching the dancers. The rhythm of the drum increases as the dancing procession comes full circle. NEBE is seated in front of her loom, weaving. ODOZI is seated on the ancestral grotto mending his palm-wine climbing rope, and at the same time, acknowledging them and taking salute from the ritual procession to mark the Iwu Festival. This is signified by the boiled cocoa yam which he scrapes with a long knife in his right hand, while invoking the ancestors in the spirit of the [3]"Iwu Festival" to usher in the new year. Then, suddenly from the rear, in a frenzied dance of possession, a man takes over the arena as the tempo of the music is heightened. The people reinforce his dance with praise-chants and invocations. He acknowledges the praises with his body, especially his chest, arms and legs, that are now quaking towards the grotto. IDA BEE and AMAECHI watch the ritual with great admiration until they recognize the lead dancer—he is MOMAH. The ritual procession continues with music and dance. The whole community emerges in shock as they apprehend IDA BEE and AMAECHI, who in turn, try to retreat further into the grotto/shrine. Once MOMAH recognizes the strangers, he throws away his [4]"Ukpa" in anger. Silence.*)

ODOZI:
  Who are you?

IDA BEE:
  (Uneasy.) I am IDA BEE. And this is my son, AMAECHI.

ODOZI:
  Where do you come from?

IDA BEE:
  We come from Milwaukee.

ODOZI:
  Mi-li-waa-ki? Mili—waaki ... *(Pause.)* Where is that?

8

IDA BEE:
America.

ODOZI:
America? You come here from Amilika?

IDA BEE:
We come in search of our family.

ODOZI:
In our ancestral grotto? Inside our sacred shrine?

IDA BEE:
We hope to find our family here.

ODOZI:
Which family?

IDA BEE:
Our father's family.

ODOZI:
(Turning to the community.) Does anyone here know the strangers?

CHORUS OF IDU:
NO!

ODOZI:
(Turning to IDA BEE *and* AMAECHI.*)* Did you hear them? No one knows you here. And I certainly don't know you. Do you know who I am?

IDA BEE & AMAECHI:
No.

ODOZI:
Well, if you say you are one of us, you must know me. I am the Diokpa, the oldest man in Idu. And I think I have borne witness to the birth of everyone here ... the birth of so many seasons that I should know who my own people are. *(Pause.)* Strangers, this is Idu, our homeland. Where do you say you come from?

9

IDA BEE:
We come from America, but our ancestors are from here.

AFUZUE/ODOZI:
But what lineage do you belong?

IDA BEE:
Idu ...

AFUZUE/GRIOT:
Your clan, strangers?

IDA BEE:
I told you, ... Idu.

ODOZI:
Yes, Idu. But no one comes just from Idu. Idu is a whole kingdom, made up of nine villages, nine clans. Everyone belongs to a particular clan and lineage (*Pause*.) Or ... perhaps, you mean you are from Igalaland? (*Silence.*) Yorubaland? (*Silence.*) Biniland? (*Silence.*) Hausaland? (*Silence.*) Ashantiland? Mandingoland? (*Silence.*) Fulaniland? (*Silence.*) Zululand? (*Silence.*) Eweland? (*Silence.*) Efikland? (*Silence.*) Now your silence baffles me. What does your silence say? (*Silence.*) Where are you from?

IDA BEE:
From ... from Idu ... from all of Africa. We are the children of Africa ... born in the new world. Africa is our land. We do not have to claim any particular land or country because Africa was our nation ... before the whiteman came to divide ... disperse us. So why must we limit ourselves to one country ... one state. No! The whole of Africa is our nationality. This is our land. We are the children of Africa. We come from here ...

ODOZI:
(*Laughing derisively.*) What is she talking about? Ha! Ha! Ha! (*The crowd joins his laughter.*) You children of nowadays amuse me, you know? How can Africa be one land? (*To the crowd.*) Did she say one nation? One nationality? Africa? Stranger, are you drunk? Ha! Ha! Ha! (*Taking off his red chieftaincy cap as he laughs with the crowd.*) There is nothing one won't hear nowadays ... in this new world (*Emphatically.*) *Enu Ofuu!* Ha, children! Oyibo has spoilt our land. In-

10

deed, our world is turned upside down. Now who am I to mend it? I am Odozi-Obodo alright. But who am I? What power do I have in this new world? Answer me, my people? Do I have any power to change anything? Forget it children. Enu Ofuu has swallowed us. What can we do? *(Putting on his cap again.)*

AFUZUE/GRIOT:

(Jokingly.) Continue to adjust!

ODOZI:

My son, I am tired of adjusting. There is nothing to adjust to anymore. My head is bald. Can't you see? *(Taking off his red chieftaincy cap.)* And I'm not sure you too are not tired already. But what can we do? "Ma onye afuna ko ome, omee kofua"—That is what our people say—"If one cannot fashion out how to do it, one does as one sees it". That is where we are now. That is what we are doing. *(Pause. He puts back his red cap.)* Now seriously children, look at me. What does our strange sister want me to become now? To become Yoruba? *(They all continue laughing.)* Hausa? Bini? Or what should I become? Who am I now? To start asking questions about who I am in my old age? Don't I know who I am? *(Hoarse laughter.)* Well, my people, in my old age, a stranger has come to tell me that I do not know who I am. She wants to tell me who I am. But we shall come to that later. For now, hear her. She has come to make me Hausa, Yoruba, Bini ... In my old age, I am now born again? Like the Christians, eh? *(Laughing hysterically.)* Eh, my people? You see? *(Pause. He studies the strangers again and directly lays his charge at them.)* You have learnt well, my children. Your words are sweet ... oh so sweet they can stir the heart of a nation ... the heart of the land to weep, to dance, to come together and undo our very land ... the world ... *(Pause as he studies the strangers again.)* But that will not take us far at this time. Your knowledge will take us far away from where we are now, from our cause. We have work on hand as you can see. I cannot blame you yet for not being able to understand why we have gathered here. You are Oyibo. You cannot understand us. *(Pause.)* And I can also see that the whiteman has thought you well. That, I can see. But your learning cannot help us now. And as you would guess, I did not ... never went to the whiteman's school. So what you speak about is foreign to me. You have the gift of sight. That, I know from looking at you. Look well. I am an old man. I am too old to start learning anything new ... No, not now! A man does not begin to learn to be left-handed in his old age. It does not happen that way ... at least, not in our world.

11

(Pause as he resumes his mood of seriousness, and maybe anger.)
And if you say you are from here, you must have a lineage. So which
lineage do you belong?

(IDA BEE and AMAECHI looking confused, remain silent.)

ODOZI:

Strangers, my question is a very simple one. Look, do I speak with
water in my mouth? I do not know why you cannot understand me.
(Pause.) Perhaps, "I" am the problem. I do not understand you. Nor
do I understand your mission. *(Pause.)* Now, listen. If you say you are
from Idu, you must belong to a particular lineage. *(He begins to
count.)* We have Ubulu. Ishekpe. Umu-ozu. Ugba. Akwu. Achala.
Azagba. Okiti. And we are Aboh. To which of these nine clans do you
belong? Everyone in Idu kingdom, even the poorest person, belongs
to a clan, a lineage. Everybody has a place in our land ... even ani-
mals have their specific place in our land ...

AFUZUE/GRIOT:

(Interrupting.) Except, maybe, the bat ...

ODOZI:

Yes, the bat. But I can see they are not bats. The bat is neither here
nor there. The bat's place is split between two worlds. Only the bat
cannot be placed fully as an animal that lives on air, nor can you
place it fully as an animal that lives on land. But you are not bats. You
are human. I can see resemblances. You look like us. You claim to be
one of us. And yet you do not speak our tongue. You do not understand us, we do not understand you. Why? Because you speak
Oyibo—the white man's tongue. You talk like them, not like us ... not
like anyone in our world. And if anyone were to ask me, I would tell
them, that you are Oyibo. You belong to the white world, where you
come from. And now that you insist you are from here and yet cannot
tell where you belong, I am confused ... I cannot understand. Hmn ...
your mission brings us confusion.

AFUZUE/GRIOT:

Is it just confusion? We are here to celebrate the Iwu Festival ... to
welcome the new season and say good-bye to the old year. But these
strangers have turned everything upside down.

12

NEBE:

Now see what they have done to our entire ceremony. Ruin! *(Pause.)* Strangers, you have come to defile our land and violate the cleansing in our rites of passage ... And look at my son. How are we going to complete his rite of passage into manhood? *(Pause.)* Strangers, you must be out of your senses! Do you realize the gravity of your offense? First, you bring your desecrated body to the grotto, treading on the face of our ancestor with shoes, here in the abode of our ancestors for whom we must wear clean, white cloth to cook their food. Now, your intrusion blocks the blessing. Ah! May our ancestors protect us from the long phallus of the white-man! *(Turning to* AFUZUE.*)* Fetch me an egg-shell to purify this land, defiled.

(Exit AFUZUE.*)*

ODOZI:

(To IDA BEE *and* AMAECHI.*)* Do not scratch the itching eye with what you scratch the itching ear. Perhaps your ears are too light for the heavy accent of my tongue ... *(Pause. It is obvious that* ODOZI *is now beginning to lose his calm.)* Now, for the last time, if you say you are from Idu, where do you belong?

IDA BEE:

I can only say what I know.

ODOZI:

(Impatiently.) And what is it? What is that you know that we do not know? Tell us. Time is of the essence to us. Time is not on our side. Our sight is failing us.The moon is fast growing down. And we must complete this passage as the sun rises ... *(Sounding more urgent.)* Now tell us. What is it that you—mere children could know that an old man like me who has been the elder, a titled chief who has been in this land for all my life, have to teach me about my own lineage? *(Pause.)* Strangers, tell us what you know.

IDA BEE:

Our ancestors came from here. My father came from Idu. That is all that my father could tell me.

ODOZI:

Your father?

13

AMAECHI:
And my father too ...

ODOZI:
Hmm ... Came from Idu?

IDA BEE & AMAECHI:
Yes!

(Silence. ODOZI *takes out his pipe, lights it and begins to smoke.)*

ODOZI:
Wonders shall never cease! *(Turning to* NEBE.*)* I have said it time and time again. I have grown too old. Age is truly a burden. I have said it, I live beyond my time. Before your eyes, one day I shall be lingering here when a white albino will come to this land and claim that my seed had fathered him ... *(He rises from the stool, threateningly.)* Strangers, you stretch our patience. And you confuse us. How can you come from ... from "Amilika" and say that your father comes from our land? How? How can that be? How does this happen? We have no relations in "Amilika". That much I can tell. And I know what I am talking about ... Only once ... maybe ... when we sent our son *(Pause as he looks at* MOMAH.*)* Yes. Only then ... We sent him there ... to bring us the benefit of the white man's world who had conquered us. We sent our son so that we can learn his ways to arm and strengthen ourselves with better knowledge. As we all know, this new world has a wide mouth. "Enu-ofu."—The new world. It is fierce, it is hungry and about to swallow us. And I told you all, my people, that we must be prepared; to know it, take what best it has to offer to enrich our own world, and spit out whatever else there is in it that will poison our stomach. That is why we sent our son, MOMAH to the white man's land to open our paths and eyes that we may see beyond here, and hear with our ears how the world out there can connect to us. Well, our son is a true son of our soil. He went there to the new world and opened the road. He fulfilled the mission for which he was sent. But that was many years ago. Many years ago. And he is now here with us. He left behind whatever belonged to their world that would not be good for our land ... anything that would not advance our world, he left with them. Our great son of Idu, a true son of his father *(Pause.)* ... a tree seed. You all know him, MOMAH ... my grandfather reborn ... a true seed of Meme ... Hmn, Meme ... *(Pause.)* Strangers, now you have come, you say you are from their land. And

14

you say that you came from here. And are related to us. Well, who knows? Maybe your coming will provoke our memory. *(Pause.)* Again, does anyone here remember any of our kinsmen that may be in the new world?

CHORUS OF IDU:
NO!

ODOZI:
(Turning back to IDA BEE & AMAECHI.*)* Well, you heard them. And they heard you. No one knows ... nor recalls your father. And you say your fathers came from here?

IDA BEE & AMAECHI:
Yes.

ODOZI:
Hmn ... Maybe our memory fails us. Or, is there something our fathers and mothers have failed to tell us? I do not know. All I can say is that your words trouble me. Your mission brings us concern. Strangers, we do not remember anymore ... and ... And yet, your words strike a chord inside ... your eyes reflect my ... my being ... *(Pause. ODOZI studies them intently.)* Did you say that your ancestors went from here to Amilika?

IDA BEE:
Yes!

ODOZI:
When?

IDA BEE:
Years ago ... so many many years ago.

ODOZI:
How?

IDA BEE:
Ask MOMAH.

CHORUS OF IDU:
(Exclaiming.) MOMAH?

15

(MOMAH *has turned away in anger.*)

NEBE:

My son?

ODOZI:

How? MOMAH? *(Turning to* MOMAH.*)* I know you went to school in Amilika ... but ... but that was many years ago. MOMAH ... the strangers know your name. MOMAH. Do you know them?

CHORUS OF IDU:

MOMAH?

(Silence.)

NEBE:

(Frantically.) MOMAH! Do you know them?

(Silence.)

ODOZI:

MOMAH!

(Silence.)

NEBE:

Your father calls. Answer him now.

(Silence.)

ODOZI:

Stranger, how do you know our son?

IDA BEE:

MOMAH is my son's father. *(Holding* AMAECHI.*)* He named our son AMAECHI.

*(*MOMAH *storms out of the scene in anger and shame.)*

16

NEBE:

Be gone! Evil! Day and night never meet! Who gave you birth? Even a chick knows when its own mother cackles. What have you come for? To ruin our world with your knowledge? What do you want from us?

IDA BEE:

Kinship!

NEBE:

May the gods bend your waist! My son has no relationship with the white-man. What business has the fish with a raincoat? *(She turns frantically to* ODOZI.*)* You must dispatch evil to take its own course. Let the strangers go!

ODOZI:

(To AFUZUE.*)* AFUZUE! Remove the strangers! *(AFUZUE leads the strangers away from the scene.)* NEBE! Do you see that boy's face? Don't you see MOMAH in his eyes? I saw it. I saw it. Maybe I am getting too old. My knowledge is failing. Why, NEBE, do you see the oath and prefer instead to swear by the fire? Fart does not smell in the stomach before it is broken to wind. NEBE, truth hurts, but it opens our eyes to the world.

NEBE:

Go on searching for grains of truth lost in a bag of garri! Go on! I will be the last to fold my arms when strangers come to chase my only son into the claws of the city. MOMAH has packed his bag ready to run back to the city. And you remember how long it took us to bring him back from the city? That day will be my death when the cooking pot has room enough for maize and not for yam!

ODOZI:

NEBE! It is only a dog which sees its own shadow and begins to bark at it, thinking that another dog pursues it. NEBE, if the city calls MOMAH, then MOMAH has business with the city.

NEBE:

The gods of our fathers forbid that my only son answers calls from strange lands. The city shortens roots, shooting out its long tentacles to entrap all ... squeezing juices away from source into its stinking, choking puddle. I ask you, what if on account of these strangers my son is lost?

ODOZI:

Enough! Let the wind blow so that the fowl can show its rump! What is your fear? Did MOMAH ever tell you that he had a son? And if he has one, why must he run away from his own responsibility? Does the snail run away from its own shell? Let the [5]"Nkpordu", the basket of marketwares which dangles by the fire fall if it must, and not blame the wind! Only yesterday we entered into the final rites of his passage into manhood. MOMAH should be man enough. A man who does not know where the rain began to beat him, is not likely to know from what direction to shield his head ... If the city calls MOMAH, let MOMAH alone answer the city.

NEBE:

(Falling on her knees.) Father, for the sake of all that binds us together, for the sake of his father MEME, discharge the strangers!

ODOZI:

Why must an old man like me wet his body just because your son drops his piss like a cow and cannot trace his own steps? Go, tell MOMAH to count his teeth. Go! Tell him that if he is man enough, he should be able to perceive the smell of his own mouth. And no one need tell him that his mouth smells foul. A ram which knows that its throat must be slit for ritual does not blink at the sight of a knife. It simply grunts ... No, NEBE, the fowl flees from the ground following its own fart. Go, tell that to your MOMAH.

NEBE:

(Still on her knees, and getting hysterical.) Idu come and see!! Come and hear!!! The cooking-pot has room enough for maize but not for yam. Come and hear! The gods of our land save us from strong tides that blow leprous winds across the seas to cut us off from our children.

ODOZI:

(Calmly, gently, he begins singing a traditional tune, and then holds her affectionately.) NEBE, have you lost count of the gray on my head? Does an old man sit by while the she-goat suffers the pain of labor under the leash?

NEBE:

The gods of our land! Save us! Save my son, MOMAH, from the fate of MEME—the great father, who stepped out to be initiated into manhood, hit his left foot on a stone, and ended in the hands of marauders who hawked him to sharks across seas.

ODOZI:
Who knows? MEME lives! If the wind is strong enough to bring back children ashore on our doorstep, we sacrifice in gratitude. Will it be to his honor if the part of MEME that remains, returns to beg at his doorstep? Will MEME beg the earth to step foot on it his reincarnation? What, NEBE, will MEME say to his elders? *(Calling.)* AFUZUE!

AFUZUE/GRIOT:
Eei Baa!

ODOZI:
Return the strangers.

AFUZUE/GRIOT:
Eei Baa.

(AFUZUE/GRIOT about to leave.)

ODOZI:
And tell MOMAH that his uncle and father, the one whose chest fires bullets back to the sender! The elephant whose feet dent the soul of the earth, tell MOMAH it is "I", "Adaka Obi Egbe", The one with the heart of a gun that sends for him! Go!

NEBE:
(Desperately.) No! Let them go. These strangers may be ghosts.

ODOZI:
Let them be my "ghosts of honor." Leave their judgement to the ancestors, the ones who departed before that their wisdom may guide us.

NEBE:
(Pleading, holding ODOZI.*)* Father, ever since your brother, AMAECHI, departed and you inherited me as wife as custom provides, never before has his spirit dominated our lives in the way these strangers have brought back his image to smelt the links that bind us.

19

ODOZI:
NEBE, we watch the world. Is that not your name? If it must take strangers to bring back images of what we are and what we were, then let it be. It is the one who hides the disease that the disease hides. No, NEBE! A man must be a man and bear truth even when it is brimming hot in his palm. But women like you cover wounds to fester. Try as much as one can, pregnancy erupts like a volcano. And what was covered and planted within, soon sprouts and shoots to surface. A day comes when a man must bear his [6]"Ofor," taking his destiny in his own hands. Enough—let the gods decide.

(Sudden thunder clap. Drumming and rumbling fill the air. Lightning flashes. The air is so thick, tense you can cut it. The drums continue to rumble in the air.)

Movement Three

(Before dawn. IDA BEE *and* AMAECHI *stand before* ODOZI *and Idu* people *around the grotto.* ODOZI *instructs the* AFUZUE/GRIOT *to fetch some gin and water and a gourd of herbs.)*

ODOZI:
> *(To the* AFUZUE/GRIOT.*)* Hand the strangers water to wash their faces. Perhaps they have had too much palm-wine. Their minds are clouded. We must open up their minds.

AFUZUE/GRIOT:
> Palm-wine clears cobwebs from the head and eyes. A man's tongue charged with wine releases truth in the inner recesses of his being.

(With that done, ODOZIE *spews palm-wine into the face of* AMAECHI. *Exit AFUZUE/GRIOT.)*

ODOZI:
> *(Chanting "Afa" incantations to charge* AMAECHI *and* IDA BEE.*)*
> [7]"Uke," clear the path of the journeying one!

CHORUS OF IDU:
> Iseeh!

ODOZI:
> Remove the obstacles from their way.

PEOPLE OF IDU:
> Iseeh!

ODOZI:
> Rain does not beat the vulture in its nest.
> Speak! A squirrel's child is never born dumb!

(Again, ODOZI *spews palm-wine into* IDA BEE*'s and* AMAECHI*'s eyes and mouths.* IDA BEE *and* AMAECHI *are struggling against the effect of the potion.* ODOZI *spews the potion a third time. Frustrated,* NEBE *slumps down. The town crier,* AFUZUE/GRIOT*'s gong can be heard from a distance.* ODOZI *strains his ears to hear the message, for the voice of the town crier normally relays important messages from the palace and the oracle from the gods and goddesses.)*

21

AFUZUE/GRIOT:

Kom! Kom! Kom! Idu! Open your hearts that your eyes may see! Last season, trees with thick tufts of hair were shaved by drought. Tongues of fire licked clean our farmlands. Now skies weep red tears On our streams. And oil gluts the source of rivers. Idu! Prepare! Prepare your hearts to irrigate our land that the Iroko tree may stand firm. Can the little birds flock home to roost without trees to nest? Today, when the sun wakes up, probing plants with fingers of flame, Tickling them to sweat, gather at the grotto, when the sun wakes up. Kom! It is the mouth of the goddess, Ani that speaks! Kom! It is the message! Kom! I am only the bearer-o!!! Kom! Kom! Kom!

(ODOZI and NEBE stand ruminating over the oracular pronouncement from the gods until the light dims and drums spread. Assembly of Idu at the grotto. Prominent among them are ODOZI, NEBE, AFUZUE/ GRIOT, and MOMAH who looks agitated. Directly in front of ODOZI is a talking drum with a bowl of kolanut on top of it. IDA BEE and AMAECHI have been "arraigned" before the assembly. ODOZI has a fan made from straw beside him. He soon pulls a goat-skin bag, from which he produces his snuff-box. He serves himself the snuff in his left palm, looks around for an eligible candidate to share it with, but finding none, returns the snuff-box to its pouch. ODOZI scoops some of the snuff into his nostrils which react by emitting blasts of joyful tears that sprinkle on the victims around. Next, he points at the kolanut, indicating that he is presenting it to the group to share as a symbol of their unity, understanding and solidarity. AFUZUE/GRIOT prostrates. ODOZI raises the kolanut to the sky, calls on the gods, then shares it with the men around and not their wives who by custom are forbidden from being shown kolanut in male gatherings. ODOZI breaks the kolanut and throws pieces of it to the ancestors who lie below. The people break into chant and prayer.)

ODOZI:

Our fathers. We offer you kolanut. We thank you for the seed of kolanut.

CHORUS OF IDU:

Iseeee ...

ODOZI:

We thank you for the seed of man.

CHORUSOF IDU:
Iseeee!

ODOZI:
He who has people has wealth. No matter, wealth cannot answer a rich man's call. We are mere chicks. "Ochu nwa okuku nweada." He who drives us ...

CHORUS OF IDU:
We must earn a fall!

ODOZI:
He that we drive!

CHORUS OF IDU:
Must earn a fall!

ODOZI:
Idu Kwenu!

CHORUS OF IDU:
Eei!

ODOZI:
Kwenu!

CHORUS OF IDU:
Eei!

ODOZI:
Kwenu!

CHORUS OF IDU:
Eei!

ODOZI:
Kwezuenu!

CHORUS OF IDU:
Eeeeiii!!!

23

(Idu people are seated in a semi-circle. ODOZI *picks up a lobe of the kolanut to eat.* AFUZUE/GRIOT *takes the bowl for people to pick up and chew to stimulate the discussion.* IDA BEE *and* AMAECHI *are not yet served because they are not yet defined as "friends" of the community.* ODOZI *clears his throat to begin the business of the day.)*

ODOZI:
My people, it is I, your Diokpa, eldest son of the soil who speaks. I have called you here to share with me something that fell from the sky. Last night, as the sun went to roost, a truth, red with blood, which my eyes cannot look alone, came upon us. I have therefore called you, my kinsmen and women. Our people say that he who asks questions never loses his way. Though oldest among you, I have come to ask questions. I have more questions than I have answers. The search for answers might show the inner meaning of ourselves. My people, you may have noticed foreign elements before our eyes. Strangers in our own land, you may ask? What is strange about strangers? Have we not always known strangers? Is ours not a world of strangers? Yes ... yes ... strangers we all are, and have been—always. Strangers! But some smell more of strangers than others! Sometimes, experience of strangeness recalls tastes of homecoming. And when strangeness reeks of homecoming, my own nose opens up to the truth. Before you all, my kinsmen and women, strangers stand reflecting images of us in their eyes. Where they come from? I do not know. Except the black blood which flows in them, they say, once had its origins from here, until lost to the seas. What they do? I do not know, except the truth of their search. Here they are to tell stories of the beginning, ending their search. This much I can say for now. If the strangers are of our blood, we will find out. Patience. Let the strangers speak!! *(to* IDA BEE *&* AMAECHI.*)* Trace the link. Pick up the thread that we may find the loose ends and tie the knot from this very end.

IDA BEE:
(Putting down her bag.) In the beginning, a fire raged on North Avenue, Milwaukee. A fire set by angry white men that swept through my home, trapping my mother inside the flames. Nothing was left of her besides her charred body amidst the debris. The fire had snuffed out my sense of hope. It was a night I longed for daddy to return home. Daddy was a laborer who had been laid off his job without compensation. He felt demoralized and hopeless because he could not support us. He left one day in search of work and never returned. The

24

only trace left of him was found in the debris of the fire. The "Ikenga." He gave it to me on my twenty-first birthday. For days and days, I gazed at the Ikenga, without my mother. Then one day, a knock on the door.

(Light changes. IDA BEE *and* MOMAH *are in a flashback. We are back in* IDA BEE*'s house on North Avenue in Milwaukee.)*

IDA BEE:
Who is it?

MOMAH:
Africa.

*(*IDA BEE *opens the door.)*

IDA BEE:
Who are you?

MOMAH:
I'm sorry ma'am, but ... eh ... you see—eh ...

IDA BEE:
You see what? Who are you?

MOMAH:
I'm a student.

IDA BEE:
Where?

MOMAH:
UW-Milwaukee.

IDA BEE:
What do you want?

MOMAH:
I'm selling raffle tickets for trips to Africa. Can I interest you in a trip to Africa?

25

IDA BEE:
You got any identification?

MOMAH:
Student I.D.

IDA BEE:
(Taking out the I.D.) Is this your name?

MOMAH:
Yes.

IDA BEE:
(She studies him for awhile, and lets him in.) I've never heard of an African named JACK.

MOMAH:
Well, that's what I'm called, JACK.

IDA BEE:
How many African brothers do you know that are called JACK?

MOMAH:
Not many, but there must be some. Times have changed. New influences, new beliefs, new ways. My name is JACK!

IDA BEE:
Most African names have meaning. What's the meaning of JACK?

MOMAH:
Hmm ... Well, I don't know. Don't know really ... em ... it's just a name. A name has no meaning. What should I care about the meaning of a name, anyway?

IDA BEE:
A lot, I suppose. What is your African name?

MOMAH:
Does it matter really?

IDA BEE:

It matters! It does! To me ... to us ... who are here, without ... It has to do with the true African identity. If you had been addressed as boy and called "Hey Boy! Come here"!, as if you were a dog or something, you would have understood that you had a name. A name which meant so much to you and to your world. A man who knows the meaning of his name answers to the ancestral rhythm and knows where he is going. Brother! If people attached any meaning to your name, they won't call you "Boy" at 50—What does your mother call you?

MOMAH:

MOMAH ... MOMAH.

IDA BEE:

Meaning?

MOMAH:

"The gods or the ancsestors know."

IDA BEE:

You see! Of course "the ancestors know"! It has profound meaning! They know. Why shouldn't they when ... when ... they see it all? What preceded us. What we have experienced. Where we are now. And where we are going. Why should they not know why they gave their life for the knowledge that we have now, the knowledge that cost us so dearly? And what is this—our lesson? Is it not that here in these states, the color of a man's skin classifies him as evil? And certain people, exploiting class, exploiting race, feed on nothing but evil? *(Pause.)*

MOMAH:

What part of Africa are you from?

IDA BEE:

North Avenue, Milwaukee. *(They laugh.)* How about you?

MOMAH:

The confluence of the river Niger and the river Benue. No. Bendel, really. In Benin, we call it "Beden". *(They laugh.)* No seriously, I come from the land of IDU.

27

IDA BEE:
Idu?

MOMAH:
Yes.

IDA BEE:
You don't mean it! My people came from that region.

MOMAH:
Your people?

IDA BEE:
Yes, my great-grandfather. They say I look just like him. My father told me many stories about our people, stories that gave us a sense of security in a hostile world. And here you are, JACK, standing in my home like the living image of my own father ... oh, my African brother, JACK!

MOMAH:
So, how many raffles do you want to buy?

IDA BEE:
(She pays him, but is still studying him.) Brother, I've met brothers from your region before; fine, young, robust men with a strong sense of who they were. How come you're so undefined? I mean, indefinite?

MOMAH:
Well, it's not a question of being indefinite. I mean, I come from Africa. I was born, bred, buttered and battered in Africa. This Africa you dream about is a hoax.

IDA BEE:
Meaning?

MOMAH:
It's a myth!

IDA BEE:
A myth ... ? Are you studying mythology?

MOMAH:

Urban Development.

IDA BEE:

Urban Development!? In Africa?

MOMAH:

And why not Africa? Perhaps you're one of those who think that Africans are like apes living on treetops, dancing naked all year round and eating other human beings. You are surprised that Africans develop cities and build houses, too? Yes, we strive to turn Africa into modern Europe. We gonna make it. The big cities where no one cares about anybody, each person is his own person! Independent! Alone, with scope, freedom and opportunities to make it to the top alone—away from this backward, burdensome African extended family system. Everyone nosing into everyone else's business—each, the brother of so-and-so, mother of that great grandmother from this village and all that. Ugh! African ways are so long and burdensome. American ways, so "cool" and so fast! A world of individualism and prosperity! Huge populations of skyscrapers, long, flashy, glittering cars, atomic energy, atomic weapons, and star wars. We in Africa are determined to transfer American, European, and Russian technology to Africa!

IDA BEE:

(Cynical.) Really? Interesting ... What do you hope to achieve with all this modernization?

MOMAH:

(Excitedly.) Transformation. We must acquire a new form of civilization. Transform the basis of our lives. Step into the 21st century walking tall. Modernize our culture. Americanize our ways.

IDA BEE:

And how are you gonna do that, "Mr. Cool Jack"?

MOMAH:

Anglicize our language. Indeed, get rid of our native languages and adopt civilized languages like English, French and German. Languages that flow with hard currencies and dictate the tides of international trade. Black-out the past. Our ancestors are nothing but archeological specimens for advanced studies on impoverished human species ... Black-out the black past, backward in time and space. I

29

mean, it is time we in Africa shortened our long-winded names to JACK, TOM, DICK and HARRY.

IDA BEE:

(Laughing.) TOM, DICK and HARRY in Africa! You don't really mean that, do you?

MOMAH:

MCDONALD's, too!

IDA BEE:

You don't know what you're saying. You cut off the past and you'll lose your bearings and never retrace your steps to the ancestors. Don't you know that?

MOMAH:

What in the world are our ancestors worth? Can they build planes? Jaguar? Lexus? Mercedez Benz? Go to the moon? *(Parodying.)* Ancestors! Ancestors! Oh, give me a break! Our ancestors should just sleep fine in their graves. And we shall rise ... wake up ...

IDA BEE:

(Still laughing.) Oh, poor lost JACK!

MOMAH:

You black Americans are a mystery to me. You've got the best of all possible worlds. Be straight with me.

IDA BEE:

We are adrift on a foreign boat without a rudder. Losing confidence in our memory of past glory. Our minds clouded with distrust. Suspecting that the world that gave birth to us is our worst enemy. That our own people, brothers and sisters, are the ones we should fear most.

MOMAH:

You live in a world of plenty. What have you got to fear?

IDA BEE:

(She sits next to him and looks at him with admiration, even lustfulness.) Love lost.

MOMAH:
Love?

IDA BEE:
Love between brother and sister.

MOMAH:
And how does one find love that is lost?

IDA BEE:
Within. We look within to discover love. But it is hard to discover love when your spirit is drifting from the source, ... your beginnings ...

MOMAH:
I don't understand you. There is nothing in the past that compares with what you can find here in the present. Your world is flourishing. Mine is dead *(She looks longingly at him and begins to sing the blues. At first,* MOMAH *looks on, but soon starts drifting towards her and getting emotionally provoked.)*

IDA BEE:
Do you hate me, JACK?

MOMAH:
How can I hate somebody I hardly know?

IDA BEE:
I am your sister, JACK. If you cared about the African race, you'd know that and call me sister! And I would call you brother. You'd no longer be JACK, just another American boy. You'd be the man in my life, charting a course of rediscovery, for you and for me, for us.

MOMAH:
Right now, your brother needs food.

IDA BEE:
You can have food. My pantry is open to you. What else do you need?

MOMAH:
A place to sleep.

31

IDA BEE:

You can sleep here, brother. I have room for a weary man working his way through college.

MOMAH:

I'd do much better in my studies if I didn't have to work ...

IDA BEE:

(She holds his hand and begins playing with him.) I have a job, brother, not a high payin' job, but you'd earn enough to support ... your opportunity to secure the skills needed to resurrect the motherland.

MOMAH:

(Warming up to the romance.) And my seed, my father's seed. What would I do with it?

IDA BEE:

Plant it, brother, plant it! *(IDA BEE begins another tune. At first, MOMAH hums along, but soon heartily joins the rhythm. Flashback ends with IDA BEE and MOMAH in romantic embrace as the lights go down, and rise again soon after. We are back to the present.)*

IDA BEE:

And he did! As the seed grew in me, MOMAH, riding on my back, graduated from college, secured the Green Card. And with that, he went out and got a car, a house. Then I became irrelevant. He no longer needed me. Nor wanted me. His intention was to blot me out of his memory. I was pregnant. He insisted I must abort the child. Abort the past. Abort anything that would interfere with his mission to become JACK in mind and body. My brother saw no hope in the black race, in the black race born anew. And he abandoned me with a dream and a child. It was the night of Halloween. He boasted he was returning to Africa. He was going to transform Africa into a haven that even America would envy. His Africa was going to be one long city without a past, only a present! And the city would be built, not with mud or earth, but with synthetic gold! And the new people, so tall their heads would touch the sky! He called me a slave daughter with foolish dreams of a primitive Africa who was born to serve the world for eternity. Bile surged up in me. I had endured all else: hunger, racism, sexism, classism, deprivation, injustice. But certainly not a slap on my past and present. Certainly not from one of my kind desecrating my identity, our collective identity. One is better off

32

dead without identity. The blood that knitted us together swelled into my hands. I knew I had lost him. Lost him, MOMAH, forever. But I also knew I had gained a seed, the seed I must plant on firm soil. The African soil, fertilized in love, pride, and self-assurance, that fruits may abound and come to life again. (IDA BEE *turns to* AMAECHI.) AMAECHI!

(*Suddenly,* MOMAH, *who has been fidgeting, rises up to his feet, smashing the mirror which he had been clutching in his palm. The entire assembly is startled. As the glasses shatter, he lunges forward, grabbing* IDA BEE *by both hands and shaking her much as one would shake a tree laden with ripe fruits. His eyes look wild and charged.*)

MOMAH:
(*Shaking* IDA BEE.) ENOUGH! (*Pause.* MOMAH *turns, looks around the assembly, turns to* AMAECHI, *stares at him. Then father begins to pace towards son. Holds him. Looks him in the eyes, stretches his hands and spreads them around* AMAECHI, *thus enveloping him. Instantly, the assembly rises to its feet, petrified. A vibrant rhythm of drums overpowers them. As if in a reflex, they all rise and stretch out their hands towards* AMAECHI. *The music rises in crescendo as the people sing and dance.* NEBE *dashes into her hut. She returns with traditional items for* [8]*"naming ceremony" for a new born child; a newcomer. The people form a circle.* AMAECHI *is at the center.* ODOZI *administers all to* AMAECHI.)

ODOZI:
(*Performing the naming rite as the people continue singing and chanting in the background.*) AMAECHI! AMAECHI! AMAECHI! Three times I call you! Your name is AMAECHI! Who knows tomorrow? Antimony. Black whose essence is indelible!

CHORUS OF IDU:
Iseee!

ODOZI:
AMAECHI, take alligator pepper. Alligator charges lips to speak truth, to defend truth. Son, may you be the mouthpiece of your land?

CHORUS OF IDU:
Iseee ... !

33

ODOZI:
Son, here is oil. May your ways be free. Oil eases paths!

CHORUS OF IDU:
Iseee!

ODOZI:
Child, take fish ...

(Suddenly, AFUZUE/GRIOT *and* MOMAH *pounce on* AMAECHI. *As he struggles mildly not knowing exactly what they are up to,* NEBE *extends the "cord" to the thread in her loom, and then symbolically cuts the child's "umbilical cord" and makes an imaginary incision for circumcision. The "cord" is given to* ODOZI *as the living father of the family. He in turn makes a symbolic gesture by which he buries the cord at the foot of the* ⁹*"Egbo tree" in the grotto.* ODOZI *pours palm-wine libation unto the earth in thanksgiving for a new addition to the family. This is accompanied by ululation as the dance, music increases in tempo, and until the moon is half-full.)*

Movement Four

(IDA BEE, alone at the grotto. The dance and music of the last scene have quietened down, except for some distant echoes of drums throbbing intermittently.)

IDA BEE:
(Excitedly, passionately breaking into spiritual song until overwhelmed, she breaks into monologue.) My son, is at last part of the fold. And here, at the grotto, my journey ends. Or could it be the beginning? The end of the end at the grotto? Knitted with cords of black navels? Pregnant with secrets that weave the souls of my people? Secrets enshrined in the grotto where the beginning of the circle ends to reveal the essence of backness? Here, where my journey ends, I take a leap ... and I limp ... into where pain heralds the birth of a new born child. Pain, breaking the hymen for birth ... breaking soil to deliver seed. And I look at my belly and trace the thread, blood from my navel to the grotto, which perhaps someday will bind me ...

(Footsteps can be heard. IDA BEE listens, stops. It is NEBE singing as she approaches IDA BEE at the grotto. NEBE is threshing wool which she spins from a gourd under her arm as she sways and dances towards IDA BEE.)

Nebe's Song: "Enu Ebuke" ("The world is too large")
1. Isi n nwamo o o o o Oh!
   Obulu onye na kpoisi na kposi?
   Osia na nwami ife na kpoi yo o o o o
   Jezu kao kai enee
   Onye ba bienenu ne nu ebuke
   Onye ba bianu uwa o o o o!

2. Aka n nwamo o o o o Oh!
   Obu onye na kpo aka na kpo aka?
   Osia na nwamife na kpoi yo o o o o o
   Jezu kao kai kenee
   Onye ba bianinu ne nuebuke
   Onye ba bianu uwa o o o o!

3. Afo n nwa m o o o o Oh!
   Obu nu onye nakpo afo na kpo afo?

35

Osia na nwa mi ife na kpoi y o o o o
Jezu kao ka kenee
Onye ba bienu nenu ebuke
Onye ba bia nu uwa o o o o o ...

(NEBE *sings and sways to the rhythm of the song as she arrives at the grotto.* IDA BEE, *uncertain about the meaning of* NEBE*'s act, stands frozen but watching apprehensively until* NEBE *suddenly quickens, leaps and stretches the side of her palm to stroke the neck of* IDA BEE. *This act of "neck cutting" is called "Ibe ugo onu." Traditionally, "Ibe ugo onu" among the Aniocha-Igbo community is an amorous sign. It is an indication of love and romance from male to female, or as in this case, from any member of the family to a wife married to that family as an indication of the bond between them. It soon becomes clear to* IDA BEE *that* NEBE *is being playful as she smiles and repeats the "neck cutting" over and over again. Then* IDA BEE *hums and dances, following the* NEBE's *rhythm.)*

NEBE:

(Chanting.) Alua! Alua! Alua! Welcome stranger! Alua Oshimili! Ocean! Wife whose eyes sing! Eyes that glow, flashing dark waters, mingling waters with fires. Fires floating on dark waters, courting the depths of oceans in a mirage! Welcome! Welcome! Welcome wife! Alua, Asia! Asia nwa Asia ngwo! Fish and beauty-queen of rivers! Asia whose soothing skin holds elements in waters captive, while she glides her way to their soul! Welcome! Welcome! Welcome! Welcome Uli, Uli, whose blackness tattoos conscience with dignity. Welcome Alo, the black die on the weaving-bowl whose blackness, white cannot endure. And charged to attack black, white loses its color to black. Oh black! Ebony, beauty of the forest! Soul of the forest! Ebony whose dark essence mocks termites! Ebony whose body laughs aloud at the untutored hand carving the history of a land! Hand untutored in the secret mystery of a dark forest! Welcome! Welcome! Welcome Egbe! Woman ... Egbe, woman-bird who does not know a land but journeys there all the same. My fellow woman ... and daughter ... welcome to our land ...

MOMAH:

(With fire in his eyes.) Dance no more!

(IDA BEE *and* NEBE *halt. Silence.* IDA BEE *looks from* MOMAH *to* NEBE *and* NEBE *back to* MOMAH. *She is not certain whether this is a conspiracy between mother and son. So* IDA BEE *looks anxiously from son to mother and from mother to son.)*

MOMAH:

(Calmly to NEBE.*)* Mother.

NEBE:

Son.

MOMAH:

Your dance shatters the silence of the night. Night longs for sober reflections. Let silence return. Mother, you may leave us.

*(*NEBE *perplexed, turns to leave, but* IDA BEE *rushes forward to stop her.)*

IDA BEE:

(Tearfully.) No! Mother! Stay ... I need you! For once in a lifetime I feel caressed by warmth and cradled in the bosom of a motherland ...

MOMAH:

(Sternly.) If she is to be my wife, leave us.

NEBE:

(Departing.) If she's your wife, then she is my own wife, and daughter, too. MOMAH, remember these breasts which fed you, breasts which still flow from my very soul? They may look dry like oranges in the harmattan. But the milk which dried to powder, flows and drips with the saliva of the infant, with tears carved as estuaries, into a mother's heart. What does a man know about the origin of milk? How can a man measure the value of a woman's breasts? Women bear the breasts of the earth. Men must not destroy it.

MOMAH:

Enough sermon, mother! Leave us to our age! Leave us to our fate!

(Exit NEBE. *Brief silence.* IDA BEE *and* MOMAH *regard each other intensely as two roosters about to fight.)*

IDA BEE:

Well, now, MOMAH, how ironic that I should be witness to your entry into manhood when you have not demonstrated to me a single ounce of manliness in all the years I've known you.

MOMAH:

Hold your mouth woman.

IDA BEE:

Sure, just as you buried the memory of your son. Left him to find his own path in a world that had no place for him, while you chased dreams of synthetic golden cities that would stretch across Africa without traces of the bush that has just anointed you a man. AMAECHI, who is becoming the real man, has come of age without a single piece of guidance from you.

MOMAH:

Shut that wide mouth woman! Who do you think you are talking to?

IDA BEE:

MOMAH ... the master builder!

MOMAH:

Haven't you done enough damage? Embarrassing me in front of my people with a son nobody even heard of? Are not you ashamed? A woman who lays claim to marriage?

IDA BEE:

Marriage? MOMAH. I never said anything about marriage. I raised my son, and supported you too, without ever asking you for anything except to take responsibility of teaching our son the values of African manhood. But I see now MOMAH, you could never have helped me. It has taken too long for you to become a man.

MOMAH:

I've heard enough. Woman! You will do no further damage. With the powers borne in me as the son of Idu, I cast you to the bush of demons where you will become food for the gods! (MOMAH *advances to push her.*)

IDA BEE:

(Shouting.) MOMAH. You have no power over me. Here, in this land, my bond is to the earth. No knife, no matter how sharp, can sever it. My feet, they stand firm for I am a child of this land. And no matter what you do to smash the shadow of me in the past, my image shines to reflect the face of tomorrow through my son, whose umbilical cord is planted deep in the earth of this homestead, where now I am condemned to be a stranger. But MOMAH ... MOMAH, in the end, I charge you with the blood which binds us, the blood which the eternal bond of motherhood shall show your eyes to the painful truth.

(Suddenly MOMAH pounces on IDA BEE, pushing her to the forest of the demons, while she resists and fights back. The struggle intensifies, but in the end, MOMAH subdues her and pushes her into the forest. A crashing sound is heard.)

MOMAH:

Away with you, woman. Out of my sight! Into the bush where you will be fed down the gullet of the gods. As Osu you came, as Osu will you return!

Movement Five

(ODOZI *at his bellows, smelting and casting some metal into bronze.*
NEBE *threshing wool from a calabash into thread on a forked-stick en-*
ters, as she is chewing a piece of kolanut.)

NEBE:
(Greeting, genuflecting.) Ojogwu.

ODOZI:
Eei. Oliakum!

NEBE:
(In praise chant.) The one who carries the heart of a gun! Hunter and
panther who out-sprints all hares in the forest! Lion and elephant
both! The one who yawns, sending people on stampede for fear the
lion might be angry! The elephant whose sole dents the earth! Ojogwu! Uwa oma nnanyi!

ODOZI:
(Replying in chant and placing his right hand affectionally on her
shoulder.) Eei, Oliakum! Great mother of the land! Awali Ego! They
who measure money with baskets! Awali Ego! Arise, wife!

(NEBE *rises, sits on a carved stool by the forge.)*

ODOZI:
How's your son?

NEBE:
Which son?

ODOZI:
I mean your son ...

NEBE:
(Laughing cynically.) Hmn ... That which grins by day or that which
spreads its lips by night, loaded with secrets of fires that burn our
bald heads to blister ... Mocking the darkness that clothes our hearts?

ODOZI:
The yam head that sprouts to shoot ... I mean your son, NEBE!

40

NEBE:
(Sarcastically.) Ohoo! You mean the one devoured by beetles long ago? If that is what you mean, I can see no son. Only sun above whose mocking laughter drowned the dark essence of a son we once had ...

ODOZI:
You amaze me woman! How often, and how long must a man teach a woman that suns do not sleep forever? That the sun must rise in the east, journey through clouds. And though thunder may roar, and rainbow may spread its tentacles, its many rows of deceit, galloping and fleeing like python ready to prey, the sun swallowed, emerges from the anus of clouds setting in the West? It is the pattern. It is the world; changing, flowing, sauntering from side to side. Never still, never steady. The sun never journeys straight across heads in the sky, NEBE! NEBENU!! Our dear mother and wife! Open your eyes and read the bow stretched tightly across your vision that we may together blast the arrow on the zero of white eyes. Now, how's your son?

NEBE:
I have no son. Never had a son, nor ever will. Our son lost his manhood to woman whose breasts now swell with pride. Henceforth WOMAN shall be my song, for I can see through the eyes of woman today, the contorted brows of the land bearing the burden of tomorrow.

ODOZI:
Nebe, a world where woman rules is a world of dream ... Of fancied colors in the rainbow, wearing a thousand shades of Uli seed that are marked from the rays of a fleeing sun. Deny that the sun's phallus does not penetrate the inner depths of your being! Though you may wince and groan below, Man, always will lie above woman ...

NEBE:
Enough of that now! For years, the hearts of women have dangled in the pendulous swing of the ways of men. A daughter now takes the paddle that steers the canoe to the shore. The son died long ago when sun went to sleep! Now, time reincarnated, delivered a daughter in the twilight of hope. It's the land's hope reborn, delivered into the safe hands of a darkening time. And I wish I were a mother blessed with her kind. Let your son go and sleep with the sun. The sheep which boasts of a ram as its only child is childless.

41

ODOZI:

(*His lips spreading with mischievous smiles, takes up his anvil and begins to knock some torn pieces of metal together.* NEBE *is still threshing wool and producing threads that she rolls into the yoked or forked stick. Painfully, she starts singing a mournful tune but Odozi will not let her go far.*) Mother! Tie the knot of patience on the bleeding umbilicus, that its black head may heal. One must not rub out the black in the eyes because they itch. NEBE! Our great mother! After so many seasons of watching many tides swell to our shores, I thought you would have learnt that no matter their heights in the sky, waves stand crashing at the vulva of the land. And as they loose their charge, foam at the mouth and recede to their wild abyss ...

NEBE:

(*Interrupting.*) True, father. The waves recede but always leave destruction behind. Where is your son?

(*Suddenly,* MOMAH *enters the scene. He now wears a pair of jeans, and carries a heavy travelling bag which weighs him down as he leans over*)

MOMAH:

Here! Mother ...

(ODOZI *and* NEBE *startled, freeze momentarily. Brief silence.*)

ODOZI:

(*Breaking the silence.*) Long may you live! Son! You're truly the son of your father! How's AMAECHI?

MOMAH:

He lives.

NEBE:

And the mother? The new daughter of the land?

MOMAH:

Your daughter, not mine! Let's change the subject. Talk about the living tomorrow and not dwell on the effeminate past dispatched to the bush of demons.

NEBE:

(Angrily.) Hear him! Hear the foul wind that breaks from the mouth of one called son! Hear him! Idu hear!!

ODOZI:

(Alarmed.) You mean you have sacrificed her, the one reborn to the gods of our land? You cast her away as Osu?

MOMAH:

(Defiantly.) And what else? Sand thrown up to the winds returns to source. As Osu, she came, as Osu she returns. What's all the fuss about? Woman as food for the gods? The gods have always been fed with [10]"Awai" and [11]"Akasi" so that the past may retire to sleep.

NEBE:

Oh what have you done? You have sacrificed a mother to the demons of the bush who will gorge themselves with her nurturing breasts, and cause labor pains which push the future to be born deformed?

MOMAH:

My mind is made up. The woman ... your daughter had no benefit for the seeds of our future stability.

NEBE:

(Vexed.) Why must the cooking pot contain maize and not yam? If we must begin again, the present must come to terms with the past. And patch together the tattered pieces.

MOMAH:

The fragmented pieces we reject as the feet of the survivors remain poised for the future. It's the way of the world.

ODOZI:

Enough! When will you ever know yourself, MOMAH? When will you ever learn that the present must see a reflection of self in the contorted face of the past! MOMAH, you will not grow. You cannot desert your land that weeps for your soothing hands to heal her burning face, her wounded heart. No MOMAH, you cannot run away from this responsibility that we now share. How can a snail run away from its own shell? The snail feeds on itself, on its own soul, as men do, in times of adversity. But then, we know too that the rain will come after draught. That is the time to heal. A time to move forward that the

43

night does not meet us here. MOMAH, this is that time. You are the hand of time. You cannot kill it. Mother! Take away that bag from him. *(NEBE hurridly takes it away.)* Son, this is your time to be a man. A man does not go chasing after rats when his house is on fire. *(Again, Nebe breaks into song which sounds like a lullaby. Sudden interruption. AMAECHI enters the scene, his hands menacingly thrust into his pocket as he confronts his father with extreme ferocity and urgency.)*

AMAECHI:
Where is my mother? I cannot find my mother. What have you done with her? And tell me something quick before I have to hurt you!

MOMAH:
Hurt me? Your father?

AMAECHI:
You heard me. If I don't find my mother, you get hurt, JACK!

MOMAH:
How can you hurt me, your father?

AMAECHI:
I've got a gun.

ODOZI:
You would shoot your own father?

AMAECHI:
He's done something terrible to my mother. I know it. She would never leave me alone. She wouldn't just take off and leave me—not like my father?

MOMAH:
Show me your gun.

AMAECHI:
I don't have to show you nothing! Just tell me how to find my mom and I'm outa here!

ODOZI:

(Singing a brief tune to AMAECHI *as he cuddles him.)* AMAECHI! Steady yourself. Your mother roams in the bush of demons, dazed and bearing the sore bosom that nurtured you. Are you man enough to retrieve her? Or are you an infant crying that needs to cling to her breast?

AMAECHI:

I am a man!

ODOZI:

A man has the heart of a gun and would never threaten his father with malice.

AMAECHI:

I just want to find my mother.

ODOZI:

At the expense of slaying your father?

AMAECHI:

I wouldn't shoot nobody. I don't even have a gun. I was just acting like I had a gun to get my dad's attention.

NEBE:

(Still alarmed, offers incantations and sacrifices as she prays to Nzu, and offers snails to ward off Uke/Eshu, the trickster spirit at the crossroads.) Ancestors! Your children call upon you! The yoke of a new dawn. Clear the path.

(Sound of drums.)

ODOZI:

(Calming AMAECHI *down.)* Ah! It is the call to masquerade. A time to awaken the past from the lethargy of sleep so the future may be reborn with the dawn of hope. You are the light AMAECHI. We will follow.

*(*ODOZI *carries the Ikenga near the center of the forge.)*

45

Movement Six

(At the Grotto. Seated on a wooden ancestral stool is ODOZI *now dressed as a high priest ready to perform an important ritual of the land. The talkative rhythm of the last scene has now been overtaken by the reflective tune of the flute. Time is just before sunrise with doves cooing in the background.* MOMAH, AMAECHI *arrive at the foot of* ODOZI. *They are also dressed with white-wrapper loosely flowing from waist down to the ankles and with beads decking their ankles, wrists, necks and chests in the manner of Edo princes bearing shallow wooden-mortars—"Okwachi", which contains an effigy of the owner with oil, cocoa yam, salt, etc. They kneel.* ODOZI *carries a fan made from either the feathers of a peacock or multicolored feathers from various birds.* MOMAH *lifts up his own "Okwachi" (his wooden bowl of destiny) to the heights of the grotto. He motions to* AMAECHI *to do the same and he obeys.* ODOZI *now with a far-away smile like a god pleased, nods his head and commences the ritual as he sings.)*

ODOZI:

Our fathers! Light of beacon which shines before us that we may see. That we may not tread the path on a day the earth thirsts for blood. Your children, with their own hands bring the burden of destiny before you. Okwachi, the bowl of destiny that they may be filled with Nzu—the clay which molds and beautifies life. Breathe life into them, ancestors, that through them, the land may be renewed!

(Drums intone as if to put a final seal on the prayer. ODOZI *takes an egg from the Okwachi and breaks it at the grotto. As she prays,* MOMAH *and* AMAECHI *reply Iseeh,* AMAECHI *is visibly anxious.)*

ODOZI:

Ancestors your children come to you as new born. Clear their path. Here is an egg. They offer snail. Snail is for sacrifice that roads may clear. Clear their paths. Clear their heads. Clear their eyes. That they may see their inner self renewed and realized ... That they may stand towering high as Iroko in the forest of the world. That your children, wearing the solid heart of ebony, king and shade of trees in the forest, may tower high above all else. Ancestors, stretch your hands of gold. Ancestors, show them the ways of the land.

(ODOZI *offers kolanut as the bond between the living and the dead. Having offered the first lobes of the kolanut to the ancestors, he chews on a lobe and offers the remaining two to* MOMAH *and* AMAECHI *who eat in unison.*)

ODOZI:
Our fathers! The ones gone before us. It is me, your son. The hand that mends, who calls. The hand of the old. Together, join the hands of the old and the new, going and coming at your grotto. *(ODOZI holds together the right hands of* MOMAH *and* AMAECHI.*)* Ancestors! Bear witness. The old must pass away that new plants may take root.

(ODOZI *lifts up* AMAECHI's *hand, and places it firmly on the hands of* MOMAH. *Momah wears the mask. This complete,* ODOZI *rises and begins to walk backwards.*)

ODOZI:
(Chanting.) Here now, the sun rises, urging night to sleep. The sun rises, urging night to sleep. The sun rises, urging night to sleep. The east wakes up, urging west to sleep.

(As ODOZI *recedes, one hears echoes of xylophon and drum mixed with wooden gongs in the cloudy atmosphere of dawn. Exit* ODOZI. MOMAH *rising and standing face to face with* AMAECHI. *Suddenly, there is a clatter of sounds from the sky. Light flashes, thunder roars vociferously like that of an angry lion. The living at the grotto subdued and frightened are utterly prostrate. The clattering diminishes to rumbles around the grotto. A voice, ancient and deep fills the atmosphere.*)

VOICE:
Son! The stomach of the gods rumbles in pain! For thousand seasons, tumorous injuries inflicted on their children. For thousand seasons, unredressed. Empires of injustice born and nurtured on black blood. For thousand seasons, pain irrigated by my children's tears. MOMAH! Pain irrigated by black and brown earth to irrigate the white ego? How long must black and brown eyes lose their color to the red of white? How long? How long? MOMAH! Answer me!!

(MOMAH *and* AMAECHI *are startled.* MOMAH *staggers to one side. Thunder blares again, sending* MOMAH *and* AMAECHI *down, prostrate again on their belly. Their lips shut up with another thunder clap.*

47

MOMAH *holds his son like a hen tucking her young ones under her wings for protection. But surprisingly,* MOMAH *merges into* AMAECHI, *and thus as they are joined, they both look like one person with two faces/heads. It appears that this "fusion" by* MOMAH *sends the voice into an uproarious laughter which now replaces the thunder. Lightning flashes draw lines in a zigzag form across the clouds, shaped in the image of the land in the sky.*)

VOICE:
> *(Still with mocking-laughter.)* He even wants a son!!! Ha! Ha! Ha! Haaaa! Momah. You want your son?

MOMAH:
> *(Lips quivering.)* Yes.

VOICE:
> I see! MOMAH. You want your son.

MOMAH:
> Yes. But who are you?

VOICE:
> *(Angrily.)* He wants to know who speaks! Oh! Hear him! He wants to know. Did you ever want to know anything? *(Mockingly.)* Why now, you who gloated on marmalade, and jam and cheese, squashed from apples of your manhood? MOMAH, are you still a man?

MOMAH:
> *(Stammering.)* Ye ... ye ... yes.

VOICE:
> *(Mockingly.)* I see. MOMAH, you say you are a man. Who is the great father?

MOMAH:
> MEME!

VOICE:
> Hmm! Where is he now?

MOMAH:
> Dead.

VOICE:

Who killed the great father?

MOMAH:

I do not know for sure. Only, I hear stories.

VOICE:

Stories? Confirmed or rumored? What did you find out, you who call yourself a man? How did your father die? Plucked by the white hand, and chewed as sugarcane?

MOMAH:

I still do not know.

VOICE:

Ha! Ha! Ha! The illustrious son of Africa does not know how the great father died. *(Pause.)* Who killed the great father, MOMAH?

MOMAH:

Only the gods know ... only ... I ... I do not know.

VOICE:

Where is the great father buried? You! You! Oh you illustrious son of Africa. Show me the great father's grave.

MOMAH:

I know not ... Cannot ...

VOICE:

(Angrily again.) If you were your father's son, you would dig out his spirit. If you were a true son of the great father, you would walk bold. Search through mangrove and ebony and obeche and iroko. And oh— you black son! You would walk tall in the forests. Trampling down vipers and scorpions across channels of red seas. For the forests belong to you. For the seas belong to you. For the earth belong to you. Oh you! You? You, son of Africa!! Do you know yourself?

MOMAH:

But who are you?

VOICE:

(Assertively.) I am "I".

49

MOMAH:
The "I"?

VOICE:
Who are you? Where are you now? Where are you coming from?
Where are you going? Do you know yourself?

MOMAH:
I am MOMAH, son of AMAECHI. But who is "I"?

VOICE:
(Sternly.) Now leave my son! The father come back ... born again. Let
the son grow to mend and move the land! Leave my child alone!

(MOMAH *obeys. Suddenly, a moment of transition.* AMAECHI *emerges
from* MOMAH's *shield and has become the mask which his father was
wearing. Still,* AMAECHI's *feet tremble and are unsteady as he stands,
gripped with fear. At this juncture, drums begin to throb in the background. Light intensifies gradually until the final moment of transition
when* AMAECHI *turns to his father questioningly.* MOMAH *reflects on
the question, with the new image of his son without neither answer nor understanding. He trembles and covers his face in shame.*)

MOMAH:
But ... but who are you?

VOICE:
(Sternly to the new spirit of AMAECHI.*)* Ha! Ha! Ha! Who am I?

MOMAH:
You ... you are MEME, the great father ...

(*Sudden thunder-clap and flashes of lightning followed by an amalgam of
vibrant sounds of drums, flutes and xylophon. A sudden flourish of music,
mixed with flashes of tremor, as the ancient voice now transforms into a
towering figure, bearing an ancient lantern. The figure is a masquerade.
The masquerade can be played by* ODOZI. *The masquerade dances ma-
jestically to the rhythm of the drums.* MOMAH, *now completely overwhelmed with fright, withdraws, coiled up. But strangely enough,*
AMAECHI *boldly looks with curiosity at the masquerade and soon begins
to walk steadily towards it, and even attempts to touch it.*)

50

VOICE/MASQUERADE:
(Calmly.) I truly see the eyes of tomorrow in the youth of today. I see the black eyes of tomorrow beyond the white of today. *(Sharply to* MOMAH.*)* MOMAH!

MOMAH:
(Springing to his feet, and gathering sand as he rises.) Here I am!

VOICE/MASQUERADE:
Your manhood dangles in the forest of evil. Your manhood drifts apart. Gather it. Look in your arms. What is it you hold?

MOMAH:
Sand.

VOICE/MASQUERADE:
Son of Africa, sand, sand, sand in you palms. Son of Africa, treasure of sand! SAND! The fruits of yesterday and today buried in the sand. Embers turned to ashes in your palm.

(AMAECHI is now so close to the masquerade. He touches the ancient figure.)

VOICE/MASQUERADE:
And your sister, the beautiful black sister. Where is she now?

MOMAH:
She has run away.

VOICE/MASQUERADE:
(A mocking, hoarse laughter from the spirit as he gives AMAECHI *the ancient lantern.)* Trace the lost path. When you find it, return home. Fortify the grotto. Above all, retrieve the spirit of a mother, chased like a hen into the night to cackle, until if finds eternal rest in a murky pond. As long as a child is connected to the navel of a woman, it will always have strong roots. *(Calling in a threatening voice.)* MOMAH!!

MOMAH:
Here!

VOICE/MASQUERADE:
Do you know me now?

MOMAH:
(Stammering.) You ... you ... you are ...

VOICE/MASQUERADE:
Bite not your tongue, you who have eyes, but cannot see! The one who stands ahead of you, your son, AMAECHI, bears the eyes of to-morrow, filled with the light of the great father, shining to reveal the beautiful essence of black. MOMAH! Your son, AMAECHI, bears the light! Hand over the secrets of our lands, mangled in your palms that the young may fashion paths anew. MOMAH! MOMAH! MOMAH! Three time I call you. Where is my daughter? The sister that the gods sent to you? Where is the great father?

MOMAH:
[*Pause.*] Lost!

VOICE/MASQUERADE:
Where?

MOMAH:
In the dark!

VOICE/MASQUERADE:
No, MOMAH! You must find the light. It is I ... I ... I ... , the spirit of the great father. MEME, I your father. Sentenced to roam the path of darkness until you gather the fragments of light in the sun, MOMAH. And mend the split-images from the past that casts shadows on today and tomorrow. Seize the light, MOMAH! To the grotto return!!!!!

(The VOICE/MASQUERADE, *lifting and showing on his right hand, split-images of the "Ikenga," and until he dances away from the scene, leaving* MOMAH, *alone.)*

Movement Seven

(Full-moon. MOMAH *alone, ruminating and singing about the events of the last movement until the words break out.)*

MOMAH:
Each day that passes becomes more and more incomprehensible to me. Who would have told me? My father ... Was that really my father? But my father died long ago! At least so they said. My father lost on a night he was returning from the grotto after the rites of manhood. Then came the foreigners who swooped like hawks on our village and devoured my father ... *(Brief Silence.)* I see ... I can see now ... *(Emboldened, he begins to walk towards the hut.)* I must see ODOZI, the one who locks the secrets of the past in his finger tips.

*(*MOMAH *arrives in front of the hut and finds* ODOZI *polishing an image of the "Ikenga" he has just cast in bronze. Before* MOMAH *speaks,* ODOZI *has already apprehended him and begins talking to him lightheartedly.)*

ODOZI:
MOMAH! So you are here already?

MOMAH:
Yes, father?

ODOZI:
You are truly the son of your father!

*(*ODOZI *lifts up the bonze-image, looking up to it admiringly, and then hands it over to* MOMAH.*)*

ODOZI:
Well here it is! Only a moment before you arrived, images of you cast a shadow on my mind. Here it is! Right in your hands, flashing and glittering in enduring forms. You can now see your reflection. Images of you, renewed now that you are a man. Look yourself anew, cast in bronze, not in wood. A new generation of black steel tossed in gold. Take it! Let the world see through you now that you are a man.

MOMAH:

But father, I have just come from the grotto. I cannot truly retell nor even reconstruct truths revealed at the grotto. Soon after you departed, the voice and image of our great father appeared and gripped me ... us ... my son and I; tearing the dark, unveiling the shadow between us; revealing images split like this ... this that I hold, but do not have. (MOMAH, *lifting the bronze-image.*)

ODOZI:

You have ... you truly have ... for these are yours, charged and recast that the fragments may come together. For the inner essence strengthened to gather together ...

MOMAH:

But he charged my son, AMAECHI, with the lantern ... the lantern, oh so ancient that is now modern!

ODOZI:

(Smiling knowingly.) Again I charge you. Let not images of you fret in the wind. But weigh fortunes with the strength of a man. Your son, AMAECHI, holds the light that you may see far into the dawn emerging from the night. *(Suddenly calling.)* AMAECHI! *(Silence.)* AMAECHI! Come here!! Your father calls!

AMAECHI:

(Running into the scene.) Here, father!

ODOZI:

Night comes upon my eyes. My back bends to the rhythm of the sun like a drooping-orange on a homeward journey westbound in the sky. Stand together! (AMAECHI *and* MOMAH *obey,* ODOZI *gives the lantern to* AMAECHI. *He plucks some roots and hand them over to* MOMAH.) Son, you be the lantern! (AMAECHI *nods.*) Son, you are the root of our soul. Go forth, and heal. Mend our world. Mount a search into the unseen, that you may see what lies beneath the pith of our essence. To the grotto, RETURN!!

(MOMAH *finds* AMAECHI's *hand. They both turn in the direction of the grotto. Lights increase in the grotto as they arrive. They begin their search.* MOMAH *stops, relieved as if he has now found the object of their search.)*

MOMAH:
Son, I am home now. In my universe, all that we need is before us.
Behold, our fatherland, our universe! You, my son, are the seed,
AMAECHI. AMAECHI Uli!. That is your name. Uli, the plant seed
our mothers and fathers used for tatoo. Uli, the seed of that makes
the black essence. Uli, the secret of our blackness. Uli! Uli! Uli! I invoke your name, Uli. I invoke our black essence in sun, in rain!
Black! Black! Unchanging in our universe. We have all the power.
(They move to another side of the grotto.) Son, this is our universe. In
this land we have all that we need to nurture one another. And now
that I'm home, and you are here, I can now share with you some of
the secrets of our world. The secrets of healing and nurturing with
plants, roots, and herbs from this earth. Now see. *(AMAECHI
obeys.)* On this side of the grotto, the healing plants and herbs of our
soul. When your stomach burns and growls, use this plant, "Ntioke".
And there is "Aluluisi" which neutralizes poison with its compelling
essence. Next, this plant on my right, "Akuebesi", they call it. "Aku-
ebe-si"! This is the war general. Invoked with thunder, "Akuebesi"
fights battles against your enemies. True, our elders say that any tree
which finds itself in the territory of "Akuebesi" never finds good
health. "Akuebesi" smothers. Next, this one—"Inyi". Ah, "Inyi"!
The potent "Inyi"! Who dares touch "Inyi" with hands unjust, un-
clean? Who dares touch the potent one with evil hands? "Inyi"—fear
it, but use it. "Inyi" heals the wounds of the soul. "Inyi", the potent
shield! And then, this one, "Ikpai". "Ikpai"! As it sounds, run for
dear life! It is a potent weapon. It acts as a boomerang. Then "Mg-
bidimgbi" heals all wounds, especially for the tormented soul. It is
potent for soothing the nerves—for good mental health. Next,
"Isikele"! For cool stomach; for smooth skin. Son, we have it all in
our world. Our world is vast. Our world is rich. Son, this universe,
this forest is yours to use ...

*(Suddenly IDA BEE is seen emerging from the woods, that is, behind the
grotto, with a bundle of wood on her head. She mutters and sings to herself in the manner of a mad woman. She looks completely disheveled.
From another side of the forest, that is, still behind the grotto, NEBE
emerges rather frantically. Her looks show that she has been searching for
too long. IDA BEE stops and sets her burden at the foot of the grotto.)*

NEBE:
(Heaving a sigh of relief.) Daughter, you are back. Steady yourself!

55

IDA BEE:

(With a far-away smile.) Birth. Sand. See the harvest? *(Acting crazy now, she scoops sand with her hand, letting it drop slowly with relish. She begins singing a dirge.)*

NEBE:

(Upset, she takes away the bundle of wood from her.) No child! The wood cannot be your harvest. It's a bad omen—to be carrying bundles of wood. In dream, a bundle of wood signifies death. Wood is the symbol of a casket, only good enough for termites and maggots. No child! You must live as one of us. Sing me a song of life. Sing no dirges now!

IDA BEE:

(Sings a familiar blues tune. NEBE is highly upset. AMAECHI is frantic, while MOMAH looks down-cast. Her song over, IDA BEE, has a far-away smile and speaks and dances before the befuddled group surrounding her, but she still plays with sand.) Oh my life song? I'll sing you the song of the unborn child I found in the woods. I am a baby left to rot in the woods. I am the baby in the woods. I want to be born. I want to be born. Are you ready for a new birth? Are you ready? Do I smell like wood or woman?

(IDA BEE stands almost stripping and washing herself with sand. She produces the half-image of the Ikenga her father had given her and begins to pour sand on it as she sings.)

IDA BEE:

Wood is sand. I bathe myself in the sand. Wood and sand.

NEBE:

(Despairing and accusing MOMAH.) See the destructive handiwork of man! How I wish I knew it would come to this. MOMAH! Oh! It's MOMAH's doing. MOMAH's heart is bitter. Bitter as [12]"Adu"! Why? Why MOMAH did you throw our jewel into the evil forest? MOMAH, do you see now the product of your self-destruction? [NEBE *breaking down in tears*.] You snatched from my breasts this daughter I never had, but longed so much to have. Where are you now, MOMAH? Where are you to drink from the vial of your bitterness?

56

(AMAECHI, *no longer able to contain himself, breaks loose from his father who has been trying desperately to stop him. AMAECHI attempts to hold* IDA BEE *who, lost in her frenzied strange world, now dances.* NEBE *simultaneously grips* MOMAH *by the waist. The two freeze while* AMAECHI *and* IDA BEE *confront each other.*)

IDA BEE:

No! Don't touch me! The unborn must not be born.

AMAECHI:

Ma! Stop all this!

IDA BEE:

Who calls? Oh, the voice that got lost in the wood? Are you the one buried in the bush? (IDA BEE *starts running back into the forest.*) Can anyone find my face carved in the wood?

AMAECHI:

(Painfully crying after her.) Please Maaaaa! It's me, AMAECHI.

IDA BEE:

(*She stops. And in her delirium, she brandishes the "Ikenga" and looks at it admiringly.*) I am wood ... carved with a half face ... lost in the bush. Did anyone find my face carved in wood? Did anyone find it? The missing face? The missing face? Deep in the bush ... black with night? My daddy's face? Daddy's face, all buried in the sand? Buried in this sand. Where is my face? Missing? Where is my face?

(IDA BEE *lifts her bundle of wood again and attempts to run. She falls. She becomes more and more hysterical, screams, and almost loses herself until* AMAECHI *picks up a plant beside him. He squeezes the "mgbidingbi" leaves, quickly rubs the potion across* IDA BEE'*s eyes.*)

AMAECHI:

(Spewing the potion into her eyes.) It's over, Ma. You're back, Ma. This is our universe. We have the plants and seeds to heal and nurture our spirit. We're home now, Ma.

(*She stops, slowly recovering herself. The half-Ikenga has dropped from her.* NEBE *disengages herself from* MOMAH *and picks up the half image. She looks at* MOMAH *inquiringly.* MOMAH *approaches, studying the image.* IDA BEE *is sane again. Brief silence.*)

57

NEBE:

Whose image is this?

IDA BEE:

(Now calm and very conscious.) My father's.

NEBE:

Your father? Who was your father?

IDA BEE:

MEME. MEME, my father.

NEBE:

(Lost in her thought.) ME-ME ... ME ... ME ... ME ... ME ... ME. Your father? (Slowly the music "Meme" again begins to swirl in the background.) MEME? Your father? But how did he go?

IDA BEE:

MEME, my own great father. Kidnapped. Snatched. Robbed of manhood. Snatched by strange hands on the night of initiation to manhood. In the struggle that ensued, the great father's symbol was split—one half lost. But the other, he carried with him. And he handed to me as a LE-GA-CY.

(As the truth begins to dawn on MOMAH and NEBE that this story of "Meme" sounds familiar, NEBE wails and screams. AFUZUE/GRIOT and the rest of the community rush to the scene. They look alarmed. NEBE begins to sink to the ground, cupping her hands around her head in the manner of one wailing. AFUZUE/GRIOT orders MOMAH to fetch the legendary half of the face of the "Ikenga" in the grotto. MOMAH chastened, runs to the front of the grotto, producing the other half of the "Ikenga" that belonged to his great grandfather "MEME". AFUZUE/ GRIOT now takes up the narrative in the background. The people listen in dismay. The "half-Ikenga" was left on the footpath on the night of MEME's captivity. AMAECHI too lifts the new image cast in bronze, as MOMAH matches the two faces together, thus, sending his mother NEBE into a final act of hysteria as she screams.)

NEBE:

ME-ME! ME-ME! MEEEMEEE. MEEMEEE!!

(Her screams invite ODOZI. She grips IDA BEE as she wails. ODOZI understands the message as she watches the image joined by MOMAH, who drops it as soon as the truth is now obvious to him. MOMAH grips IDA BEE in his hysteria. They're both interlocked in each other's arms.)

MOMAH:
(Gasping.) Sister!

NEBE:
My daughter! ME-ME ... ME ... ME ... , IDA ... BEEE!!

ODOZI:
(Reaches out to support NEBE who appears to be fainting.) Ah! This is the day! Wife! Child! Father! Son! Daughter! This is the day! It's our dawn!

(AMAECHI still holding onto the bronze-image, lifts it up slowly, smiling. NEBE recovers and walks over to the loom. She sits down and begins to weave. IDA BEE slowly disengages herself from MOMAH. She walks over to join NEBE at the loom. The two women begin weaving together. People break into the song, "Meme". ODOZI finds MOMAH's hand, and MOMAH takes up AMAECHI's. The men form a semi-circle around the women as they weave. AMAECHI and MOMAH lift the matching faces of the "Ikenga". Drumvoices rise as AMAECHI lifts up the "Ikenga" slowly, slowly until it attains a final height. Idu voices erupt into song, and they dance. Light increases until it reaches full blast. Then fades into bluish green as at dawn. The stage lingers on with music. Floodlights.)

Theme Song of the Play: "Meme"

LEADER: Akwa Oje nisi O

CHORUS: Meme O
Oyi ke kwenu Meme O
Memo O

LEADER: Eze di no nu O

CHORUS: Meme O
Oyi ke kwe nu Meme O
Me me O

LEADER: Ije di nukwu O

CHORUS: Meme O
Oyi kekwenu Meme O
Meme O

LEADER: Meme Osia - O

CHORUS: Meme O

LEADER: Meme Oyim

CHORUS: Meme OO

LEADER: Meme Baaa O

CHORUS: Meme OO

Translation of the play's Theme-song: Meme

(a dirge, from the Aniocha-Igbo folktale, "Meme")

LEADER: Even the wrap around his head.

CHORUS: Meme O
He looks too much like Meme
Memo O

LEADER: The teeth in his mouth?

CHORUS: Meme O
He looks too much like Meme
Meme O

LEADER: His gait? His feet? His Walk?

CHORUS: Meme O
He looks too much like Meme
Meme O

LEADER: Meme, our beloved

CHORUS: Meme O

LEADER: Meme, the great Mother

CHORUS: Meme O

LEADER: Meme, the great Father

CHORUS: Meme O

LEADER: Meme, the beloved Brother

CHORUS: Meme O

LEADER: Meme, the beloved Sister

CHORUS: Meme O

LEADER: Meme, the beloved Friend

CHORUS: Meme O

LEADER: Meme, our life, our world!

CHORUS: Meme O!

**The last stanza of this dirge to be repeated many times.

Glossary of Terms

1. Ogwa: The reception hut in the traditional Igbo compound.

2. Ikenga: A wooden staff and shrine, signifying manhood, and great personal achievements.

3. Iwu Festival: The annual communal festival of renewal and cleansing in Ogwashi-Uku, Nigeria.

4. Ukpa: Hand-woven basket, made from strong canes and structured into oblong shapes with two handles.

5. Nkpordu: Hand-woven basket made from straw, for the storage of soup condiments.

6. Ofor: Ancestral staff, signifying manhood.

7. Uke: The trickster-spirit, dwelling on the crossroads.

8. The traditional items for naming the new born are: kolanut, alligaotor pepper, dry fish, salt, oil.

9. Egbo tree: A tree is usually regarded as sacred. It is therefore traditionally used for creating, marking and ensuring boundaries/borderlands.

10. Awai: Yam mashed in palm-oil. This is used for ritual by farmers in preparation for planting the season's crops.

11. Akasi: A Cocoyam species. This is used for rituals at the Iwu festival. Akasi is the favorite diet of the CHI, one's personal god.

12. Adu: Bitter-cola. It is used for ritual, ceremonies, and entertainment.